W9-ACI-998

Kingdom of the Instant

Poetry by Rodney Jones

The Story They Told Us of Light (1980)

The Unborn (1984)

Transparent Gestures (1989)

Apocalyptic Narrative and Other Poems (1993)

Things That Happen Once (1996)

Elegy for the Southern Drawl (1999)

Kingdom of the Instant (2002)

Kingdom of the Instant

Rodney Jones

Houghton Mifflin Company

Boston New York

2002

For information about permission to reproduce selections from this book,
write to Permissions, Houghton Mifflin Company, 215 Park Avenue South,
New York, New York 10003.

Visit our Web site: www.houghtonmifflinbooks.com.

Library of Congress Cataloging-in-Publication Data
Jones, Rodney, 1950–
Kingdom of the instant / Rodney Jones.
p. cm.
ISBN 0-618-22417-3
I. Title.
PS3560.O5263 K56 2002
811'.54—dc21   2002075938

Book design by Melissa Lotfy
Typefaces: Minion, Erbar

Grateful acknowledgment is made to the following publications, in which
these poems originally appeared: *The Alaska Quarterly Review:* "Keeping
Time." *The Atlantic Monthly:* "Channel." *Five Points:* "Five Walks for the
Nineteenth Century," "Going," "Ten Sighs from a Sabbatical." *The Georgia
Review:* "Divine Love," "Moses." *Meridian:* "Macabre Etude." *Oxford American:* "A Country Legacy," "Family Mattress," "Homage to Mississippi John
Hurt." *Poetry:* "The Harvest King," "Pompadour." *River Styx:* "Smoke." *The
Sewanee Review:* "Backward," "Fidelity." *Shenandoah:* "A Whisper Fight at
the Peck Funeral Home." *The Southern Review:* "Brains," "Nudes," "A Photograph in an Old Anthology." *Third Coast:* "Small Lower-Middle-Class White
Southern Male," "Wood."

"Nudes," "Moses," "A Photograph in an Old Anthology," and "Small Lower-
Middle-Class White Southern Male" appeared in book form in *Manthology.*

Printed in the United States of America

QUM 10 9 8 7 6 5 4 3 2 1

For Gloria, Alexis, and Samuel

But at my back I always hear
Time's wingéd chariot hurrying near.

— Andrew Marvell,
    "To His Coy Mistress"

It don't mean a thing if it ain't got that swing.

— Duke Ellington

Contents

One

Keeping Time

To be in there with it, tock to its tick, mud
to its chink, oh, but running, unthinking,
alive, lurid, unprepossessing, liquid,
mercurial, lucky scalpel, leap,
love cry, music sticking from the violin.

I said it, oh, and then it said to me: no
more leaden introspection, have foot
and no boundary, no second choosing,
but this thought here going, too late—
tailwater of its pure, untrammeled flowing.

Downtime looms in the mouths of statues.
Slow time looks back. Change screams,
The docks are all empty, the ships gone away.
In the sea there, bobbing and being immersed.
Why loiter over the petri dish's bloom?

Why linger? Why why when when wicks
the flesh right off the bone: what
curl and sheen of unbridled delirium takes?
How imagine *otherwise* lifted and set down,
the solid crock and rabble of other years?

This one here, now, well put: where did I
forget? Where trial gulped its long
meal by drummed and finger-fiddled desks.
Why excavate *recite* and not *compose*,
the static fact and not the moving spring?

When did kiss go? When flower power?
Why when when where shows mold-wallows
of hard and tender raptures, gene pools
place held: cinder stones beside a track.
Pick one up and throw it at the train.

The quick and slow go side by side.
What will get the girl to the dance?
Bluster or trudge? And what do you do
with your hands while making love?
The elephant circle? The tour de corps?

The luminous moment continues to grow
freshets of everlastingness, the flow
here unarchived in the only place
life possibles out of unlikelihood,
shrinks from being, leaves only thought.

Snakeskin on the doorsill, reliquary
in which all forms of nudity contrive
when the thing has wriggled on,
grown gigantic beyond losses
and gains: 1967 and 1981. Reckon,

bog down in corrections, or reanimate,
this time with a tad more spice
in the curry, a seven instead of a five.
Drumroll this desk: letters, a map
of the hot fishing spots in the lake

4

where Richard Nitz, gay-basher,
threw Michael Miley's axed-off head;
empty cigarette packs; *Praise God
I'm Satisfied* by Blind Willie Johnson;
and a telephone on top of it all.

But event resists the word. It
happened earlier, a shining thing
among reschedulings and cancellations,
late March, sunlight on daffodils,
the stab wound of "Auld Lang Syne."

Tongue knowledge needs grunt and sigh.
Who need remark much on why
the mating cardinal's *oh mama*
brings a snatch of the hesitation blues?
To see two things at once is one thing.

Not genius, work. The night is coming,
sweet hour of prayer. Shall we
bring in the sheaves, gather
at the river? Clone a better sheep?
Here now, need you know the very bird?

Who justifies Little Richard to Beethoven?
The critique of creation is a shriek.
Slow was my downfall, but love
raised me like a lily from the ground.
Long ago, she brought me into round.

A Whisper Fight at the Peck Funeral Home

1

No balm in heaven. Bone light. Things tick as they desiccate.

Immaterial who we were. Time narrows the hide to a strap —
Everything bound leaps once, and is free forever —
decay our fertilizer,
dissolution our daily bread.

Questions. Questions. Rain out there,
between here and the mountain.
Mist for the blind interpreter,
not here yet, maybe never.

But the body gets laid out by noon.
People like to have what is missing before them.

With ashes, you always worry, Are those the *right* ashes?

Corpse, I want to ask, silent mime,
are you packed?
The Ladies' Junior Auxiliary mans the train station.
What secret did you live out of like a suitcase?

Aunt Brenda took the spectacles out of a case
and placed them on the bridge of the nose.
Uncle Howard preferred
the unexpurgated face:

the valves of grief, just barely cocked, venting
a little into the overbearing politeness —

the formal versus the demotic,
the ancient grudge of the elder for the younger,
or Aristotle and Plato
transmuted to a whisper fight,

sounding something like
kopasinkassubuk and *hipatenudinsathat,*

until I thought to go out
into the hall and thank the undertaker.

3

The Summerfords were there, and the Minters,
friends of a life in the country,
church dinners, weddings, and harvests,
children growing up and going away.

What have I grown up to hate? Some
dishonesty in myself that in others
I could not face. A "scene." A scandal.
The private moment in the public space.

It used to disturb me, at funerals,
most of the people seemed so happy—
the grandnephews grand-funking in the parking lot
and the parlor, full of emcees and raconteurs;
even the widow chuckling
as she dabbed at one eye—

everything part of some vast,
mildly brawling syndicate of hypocrisy.

4

In high school, I would scrawl in the margins of textbooks
parodies of country songs:
"Always an Undertaker, Never a Corpse,"
"The First Word in Funeral Is Fun."
But death is serious. Condolence is the joke.

The undertaker gives permanents.
He takes the bald men's hats.

Once, when I was a pallbearer at the funeral
of a homicide, I watched
an old man, squint-eyed and sunken-gummed,
lean down and with one
nail-blackened finger probe the putty over the brow
where the bullet had gone in.

At least we don't hollow them out, wind them with rags,
soak them in tar, then execute their wives and dogs
so they will not have to enter paradise alone.

5

The wisdom stories are so bleak. No strawberries.

One asterisk, from a journal:

June 17, 1994,
the words
of Dr. Eugenia Poulos, she
was about to inject me with lidocaine:

Don't worry,
I'm a good number.

And another, later that week:

The secondhand word of God
must have been a wise man wisely lying.

He has turned around since dying.

6

What is the poetry of the world?
A wound and poultice.
An eavesdropper's serenade.
A shrug at Armageddon.
An obsolete love note
addressed to the vengeful cults
of longing and respectability.
Not music, not just music;
more like abandon.
The light of a conservatory
shining in the blueprint of a ruin.

7

Buddy Pittman, the undertaker, told me,
when he was fresh from mortuary school
and still alert to the possibility
of egregious error, he worked
the night shift, alone
among the steel tables,
and one night, nearly daybreak,
a body arrived.

If there was an accident and the doctors had to operate
but knew the patient would not survive,
when they shaved the head for surgery,
they would save the hair
in a manila envelope
to send later to the funeral home.

He told me this, smiling,
with the abiding confidentiality
of one who knows secrets
sometimes leak out into the open air,
and get repeated, but he tells them
anyway, and they end up
on the Internet or in a poem,
for the world leaks.

And the corpse is always a local boy.
Had been celebrating high school
graduation, banana-strawberry daiquiris

fifty miles north,
and coming back, a head-on.
The familiar dry-county mortality.

They go out whole
and come back parts.
And you put them together the best way you can,
consulting as you work
the yearbook of the Tigers, or Devils, or Saints.

Fill in the gaps. Immaterial
what we were. The soul in heaven,
the body on earth. Labor
with putty and brush. Yeats's metaphor.
Makeup and art. All that work
for one performance and a matinee.

When Eunice came with the flowers —
the deceased was in her son's class —
she wanted a moment with the body alone.
Buddy must have waited like my students wait
as I read the poem of their life —
verdict, please, not critique. She was
a long time in there. Then said,
"You've done a wonderful job,
only Ronnie's hair was brown, not red."

8

The trick is always minimalism
and understatement, a sham

like civilization —
not the accurate representation

but one's own interpretation
modified by what one

imagines others expect,
a barely legible death

a paraphrase
of the face

most of the bereaved remember
him wearing into the home.

9

Before these words,
other words filled this page:
the aunt he never saw,
his mother's twin.

His mother. Dalliance,
encumbrance. A dot
of punctuation in the silent
history of maiden names.

His father married her,
pregnant with their second child,
on condition that she never speak
to her family again.

And that was Grandma Owen,
a vine, as I remember her in her dotage,
putting out the brown flower
of one hand.

Now I want something
that will stand for a man.

10

How strange our vision of another life,
even our own. The real life
storied to oblivion. The legend
nickeled-and-dimed by facts.

The cold eulogy works best, the painting with the fewest strokes,
the record, a verse or two, jokes
if the deceased was old, requiems for the young,
sometimes music, but never anecdotes.

He farmed and the farm got larger:
a natural Calvinist, in all things moderate,
work his middle name, husbandry his byword;
hated Wallace; admired more
than Kennedy or Lyndon Johnson
Adlai Stevenson,
that mild, unelectable man;
as an old man, loved girls, any girl,
modestly, with no trace of debauchery;

had been, in his younger days, a drinker,
a juror at the trial of the Scottsboro Boys.
What works always is silence. Never
imagine any truth desperate to be told.
Easy to love the world more than God.

11

They buried him with his spectacles off.
Closed the lid. Was.
I looked down at him. His or my bones.

I still eat at his table. For years I wore his shoes.

People like to have what is missing before them.

What temper he affected to hold.

He looked in death placid and composed as he had never been in life,
as if he had resumed thinking
the thought he was thinking before he was born.

Two

Channel

for Jon Tribble

It had come up from the night depth of the lake to bend and chatter
        the rod as it lunged
under the boat, and now it flopped in the net until I had it in a slippery
        scrimmage on the aluminum floor:
suave as a satyr's haunch, but appaloosaed with dots, treble-spined,
        and whiskered like Confucius.
And now as I pliered open the jaws, and took the hook it had taken,
        it made something like a bee-buzz.
From deep in its mouth that was white as a ping-pong ball, it made
        something like absolution;
and then it curled in the icebox, whacking the beers with its tail;
        and still, there it was.
I do not like to hurt a thing alive, even a catfish, so slow to perish
        not even Saint Thomas Aquinas
or W. C. Fields could raise the eloquence to free its killer of guilt.
        In Florida, catfish walk.
Nailed to an oak, skin peeled like wallpaper, catfish won't stop
        talking with twitches.
But what they say improves on guilt. You have to have waited many
        nights, with your face
blackening from the smoke of burning tires, and shined your light
        on a belled rod ringing
over stones and going fast into the river, to know that their lives
        mean as much as your life.
And what is your life? The bottom of a shallow place? Magnificences?
        You hold them
carefully. You listen, and they say your name in ancient Catfish.

Smoke

Some men and women are watched like fire.
For my part, I was never so famous
as when they made me token smoker
on the committee for a smoke-free campus.

No sooner than I broke from the building,
Channel Six had me miked on Tower Hill.
All that year I felt Mark Twain quoting me—
but eventual policy was a done deal:

my fellow members, handpicked from the science
faculty and the staff of the Wellness Center,
brought facts and ethics into alliance
to throttle me and spur our lawyer chair,

who'd wax ballistic when any meeting veered
from his unvarying brief of grim statistics.
This seemed disingenuous and unfair,
to squeeze only horror from an addiction

as sociable as Shakespeare and Raleigh:
nicotine, our mild Methodist opium,
anatomy of cool, jump-starter of dreams,
that left men toking through tracheotomies.

To blackball smoke was to whitewash tradition.
Blues vented jazz in smoky atmosphere.
In smoke, platforms and plays got written.
Smoker's math drags a minus sign to fear.

All die. Some at forty. Some at ninety.
Why bowdlerize the indefensible?
Far healthier now that we're outsiders.
Clothes smell better. Indoor air's less lethal.

But ice and snowstorms won't kill the power.
Pleasure's the angel of any habit.
I thought of it today, seeing the chair —
here's wishing him health, though health's a fascist.

Small Lower-Middle-Class White Southern Male

Missing consonant, silent vowel in everyone,
pale cipher omitted from the misery census,
eclipsed by lynchings before you were born,
it cannot even be said now that you exist

except as a spittoon exists in an antique store
or a tedious example fogs a lucid speech.
Your words precede you like cumulus
above melodrama's favorite caricatures.

In novels, you're misfit and Hogganbeck;
in recent cinema, inbreeding bigotry
or evolving to mindless greed: a rancher
of rainforests, an alchemist of genocide.

You're dirt that dulls the guitar's twang,
blood-soaked bible, and burning cross.
You cotton to the execution of retards,
revile the blues, and secretly assume

Lindbergh's underground America that sided
with the Germans in World War II.
Other types demand more probity;
you may be Bubbaed with impunity.

This makes some feel prematurely good.
They hear your voice and see Jim Crow.
But the brothers wait. Any brother knows
that there are no honorary negroes.

Slop: A Children's Prayer

When the hogs went to hell they sang
as from the rustling of old poems
or the twilight of orchestra pits:
We who were real are exemplary.

You wrote of us once, tired of ideas:
a language of excess trimmed,
souls rendered lighter than heat
shimmering in a scaffold of mist.

Then I saw them as they had lived:
a troll luxury, a pack lolling;
pink olives, pure ingots of appetite;
their Ave Maria grunts and snorts;

their sparse shaving-brush bristles
caked with continents of mud
as they fell on their morning slops—
like us, ever wounded and shorted.

Easy to see the hog in mean cops,
shits like Milosevic, corporations
that pump trucks full of toluene
and dispatch them south from Jersey.

The main valve loosened a smidgen
of a turn, they leak to Miami, reload
and return. This makes one see
hogs as prudent compared to men.

Hogs won't swill spent plutonium
cores or uproot lost land mines like
so many truffles — no, hogs love
what we love: buttermilk, coffee

grounds, themselves cleaned up
and dressed with a sprig of parsley.
Hog heaven's a dump: the Grand
Central of our discarding is where

hogs learn the human bargain:
a third off hog earth, and falling.
The third-grader's Earth Day drawing
is a sun hog staring down

lugubriously to revise McLuhan:
Adults! The mess is in the message.
If you don't care, or won't, hogs
care just as much. Let hogs take care of us.

A Country Legacy

So they were adopted and got down from the bus,
the oldest with hair like fire, and skin
mottled with orange, and the younger brother,
large and dark, who had been raised
by bootleggers in Oklahoma, and now
entered a Christian home: the new father
who went along with everything
planned by the new mother, who still
limped from the botched spinal tap
she had gotten birthing a stillborn child.

How happy they all were now,
in and out of the truck patches and the hay,
the oldest so good with his hands
he could dismantle a frozen wristwatch
and reassemble it so it would run,
and the younger, smart and bookish,
always smiling to agree with everything that was said.
They read Bible verses at night,
and prayed, and sang the old hymns.

But it was not right until the littlest came,
bashful, slight, always hiding his head
in his arm, but handy as his brothers,
gifted with cows, horses, and pigs,
so they prayed together, longing
for something like prosperity,
until lo there arose on the plateau
above the barn twin chicken houses,

as the mother had dreamed them,
pondy roofs the length of a football field.

They had enough to eat, clean clothes,
luxuries in the Third World or another era
when indentured childhood was the norm.
Oppression's oldest franchise is a small farm:
the fraternities and tyrannies of fields;
the calumny grandfathered in;
from sermons on the spared rod
spoiling the child to our school year's
atavistic six-week hiatus for cotton picking.

But fate has something to do with love —
what's offered above and beyond
the minimum — books instead of shovels,
two nights free to play baseball.
When others, just as poor, got more,
they settled toward crystal meth,
early death, and bewildering silence.
Blame someone, parents for instance.
You're not unjust, only American.

Right off the boat, some advance
toward Harvard and high office,
but the president's a president's son.
These brothers were never men to run.
These are the men who murder
and get capital punishment.

A Defense of Poetry

If abstract identity, philosophy's silhouette, authorless, quoted,
and italicized, governs by committee the moments
of a mutinying, multitudinous self, then I'm lost.

But let a semi loaded with bridge girders come barreling
down on me, I'm in a nanosecond propelled
into the singular, fleet and unequivocal as a deer's thought.

As to the relevance of poetry in our time, I delay and listen
to the distances: John Fahey's "West Coast Blues," a truck
backing up, hammers, crows in their perennial discussion of moles.

My rage began at forty. The unstirred person, the third-person
void, the you of accusations and reprisals, visited me.
Many nights we sang together; you don't even exist.

In print, a little later is the closest we come to now: the turn
in the line ahead and behind; the voice, slower than the brain;
and the brain, slower than the black chanterelle.

The first time I left the South I thought I sighted
in an Indiana truck stop both Anne Sexton
and John Frederick Nims, but poetry makes a little dent like a dart.

It's the solo most hold inside the breath as indigestible truth.
For backup singers, there's the mumbling of the absolutes.
Du-bop of rain and kinking heat. La-la of oblivion.

Sheep-bleat and stone-shift and pack-choir.
There is a sense beyond words that runs through them:
animal evidence like fur in a fence, especially valuable now,

self-visited as we are, self-celebrated, self-ameliorated,
and self-sustained, with the very kit of our inner weathers,
with migraine, our pain du jour, our bread of suffering.

If poetry is no good to you, why pretend it can enlighten you?
Why trouble the things you have heard or seen written
when you can look at the madrone tree?

Macabre Etude

In the beginning you took me to a cemetery
to draw the flowers that sprouted from tombs,
setting up on the monument to a soldier,
and the way we started out like that,
Kafka might have published your valentine.

But our history gestates among those stones
as I picked a place clean beside you
and wrote of a willow just as I saw it
through the winged lens of a spider web.
How glad I was then to quit the exercise

and watch you with charcoal and pad:
your trial-and-error editing of shadow,
your steady relish at the heart of craft,
and our first cravenly suspicious kiss.
This comes to me outside of Urgent Care.

Having just lopped off a gobbet of flesh
with an X-Acto knife while matting student
drawings for a show, you wag a booted finger
so lush with blood it's like the swaddled foot
of a revolutionary crossing the Delaware.

Family Mattress

It's in a permanent slump now, dry-docked
in the attic, an old, dream-battered raft,
striped as a convict, but how high it lay
mornings when I stole in to drift
down the resilient ether of its cloud

as though a schooner broke from the clods
of a field I had been hoeing, or I found,
among promises never delivered,
the risible helium of the soul
that woke in sudden divings and spinnings.

Here, too, my grandparents fell back swooning,
white-shouldered in the mercy of wings,
after conceiving my father and aunt.
To heft it now and wear it through the door
is to feel the weight of their weightlessness.

A coop smell rises. I am draped in myth
and the dried tallows and yeasts of tradition,
but set it on the floor. They will not mind,
who taught me music and setting hooks,
when I rip back the ticking to feather jigs.

Homage to Mississippi John Hurt

This morning when I went to play the scales
the strings of the guitar were so cold they might
have slept all night in the Holston's South Fork.
And the week after I bought it, while it traveled
between Herman Wallecki & Sons of Los Angeles
and southern Illinois, I dreamed
of a guitar so old it had weathered gray as a barn.
It had two necks, and when I touched
the bottom one to grab a C, the neck broke off
in my hands and wasps flew from the sound chamber.
But the tone of the strings on the other neck
was yours, old sweet-playing father.

In the late twenties, they cut a few minutes
of you into vinyl and sent you back to pick
and sing for nearly forty years in church and at parties
and to get by as a hired hand, practicing fatherhood.
Greatest of the fingerpickers, lost in dark mud,
two folkies found you in the singing vinyl
and asked, "How do you do that with a guitar?"
and searched maps of Mississippi for the town
Avalon from one of your songs, and could not find it
after all that time, so it seemed you were never there.

And what was there? Kudzu, polio, celestial darkness?
My band played Bumgilly, Nowhere, the cattle
auction, the armory in Wedowee, and our biggest gig:
the annual Fourth of July bash at the asylum.
But music has no place. "Mississippi has two cities,"

said Faulkner, "Memphis and New Orleans."
Upriver, the Vienna of the Delta is Clarksdale.
We looked for easy sevenths and found a covered
wagon drawn by eight mules, a beautiful dwarf
who leapt a rail to gulp down a crushed-out cigarette.

In the New York Public Library, on a nineteenth-century surveyor's plat,
the two folkies found Avalon,
drove to Mississippi, and asked at a general store,
"Have you heard of a musician named John Hurt?"
"Third road, turn right, house on your left, up on a hill."
So they found him on a porch and took him north
to become briefly, cogently famous and leave songs—
"Louis Collins," "Candy Man," "Make Me a Pallet on Your Floor,"
"Casey Jones," "Creole Belle" —
and return to Mississippi and die.

He was a little man, but cathedrals lit up in his hands.
When Segovia heard him, he asked, "Who is playing the other guitar?"
He darted and slurred, a syncopation, a waltz evolving to jig.
By slowing the record down and listening, a phrase
at a time, repeatedly, for six weeks, I learned
to scratch out a barely detectable rendition of "Funky Butt."
I do not like to sing, but sing, driving home from work,
sing to heal the language of its long service as a tool.

Greatest of the fingerpickers, lost in dark mud,
I do not know about the god of the fathers,
but to be born again in the tink and clong of a guitar

is better than to rot in a symphony of heavenly accountants
plucking the varicose vein of elderly harps. I know
a small man's largeness can be a pistol
in the dark, but it can also play. The name of joy is music.

Three

Backward

Mind goes that way. Not life. All yesterday
was like a siesta taken by someone else;
the day before, racked in the mobile observatory
of a car; but rip another page, swing round
a corner, ambulances start to whine; a woman
I'd just met darts out, waving like hallelujah.

Inside they were working the body very hard
that had been the man who took our photograph.
Then forward, uphill from the abyss, we nibbled
couscous with the dean, consoled the aggrieved,
and rode to the Country Music Hall of Fame
to hear Steve Earle talk about writing songs.

Backward, something perverse longs to move
the immovable, aright the fallen, put back
what got took out: train, trestle, and tracks.
Wastrel, Time remarks, you've squandered me,
as if Bluto caught Popeye on a bad day, raised
a hirsute fist, and pounced, "Now spinach this."

All there, where I come from, was high praise,
so many had gone back: the earthenware
kin we talked lonesome hours, their horses
that had dragged hogsheads from Carolina,
and a few others, great in bed or prayer.
But the family tree stopped at a whiskey still.

Inside they were working the body very hard.
"He sort of knelt," she said. "One minute

he was stooping for a telephoto in his bag.
We turned him over, he was purple-black.
One breath rushed out." Revise the dark.
Embarrassment is never far from rapture.

In my family there were perfect examples
of every phase in the evolution of *Homo sapiens*.
One uncle hunkered like Australopithecus.
An aunt aged into a pale Cro-Magnon girl,
so I recognized myself some days,
a slightly smudged but still credible Neanderthal.

But backward has its perks. The plane unlands.
I stand by the Susquehanna. It isn't life, not now,
this seesaw where the past and future swing.
Last week Pittsburgh, Nashville, then here,
the point from which I orbit and dream,
the ground control and locus loco of a life.

I say, Go past, young man. Redemption waits.
And rapture. And resurrection. The stuff
heroic prayers commanded of such gods
as might be coerced to staff the heavenly
counter marked *Complaints & Returns.*
I say, This river runs backward, Lord.

Also, cancel soon. The future's too late for me.
I'm stickered and plaster-patched with the past,
with fencerows, moo-cows, and fields' dark mire,
with bog wallows, pussy jokes, and sermon fire.

One ridge I lived. I see the bacon in the hog.
Inside they were working the body very hard.

Spring, more than a year ago, and what is that?
A little while longing and not even a sentence?
Days flash-seal with a pop like canning jars.
There was an olive in an empty martini glass.
There was the light of one place: the kingdom
of the instant against the democracy of all time.

Five Walks for the Nineteenth Century

Strip

From Gator's Automotive toward the college,
through the almost empty parking lot of the mall
shut down for the daily geriatric promenade,

I had come off the pavement and trekked
across the lawn of the discount appliance den
when the muck's shoehold at the bottom of the ditch

put me in mind of the bog round Sally Mack Creek:
the sucky mush, swamp gas, and beavered willows
where I would go in foggy adolescence,

foraging after the private gods of athleticism and romance.
And now came the small trance where poems
start up from the wet shoetops to get short-circuited

by a startling Camaro full of vagrant redneck kids,
or a gangsta BMW blasting Snoop Doggy Dogg.
I stood at the junction of 13 E and Lewis Lane.

Across the way, Colonel Sanders, Pizza Hut,
and the Auto Shack were also starting up
from buildings anchored in the hardpan earthfill

that had torn the salamander from its log
like the inner life varnished on a Wordsworthian page.
Coitus interruptus of the dreamlife.

The sidewalk glazed ahead, the glare and noise
of such small commerce as joins the parts
of little towns between the malls and the dead

but ever resurrectable downtown,
to be recollected in tranquillity perhaps —
or as I had invented Wordsworth, head high

in his habit of ambulatory composition, and Dorothy
behind him, copying down, when he gave
utterance to some glimmering of the soul

such as "O noble trilling streams where satyrs
leap to missive Elysian bells, O stately alders" —
a thing that went more like the world.

But back to the swamp. I felt it under me,
and in me, all scrawls of lichen, mints and springs,
that seemed the code, lost and irretrievable,

as the storefronts' emblazoned blowouts dwindled
past, and the streets shaded off to the side
to the projects where the rock curbed in the pipe,

glittered for an instant, and was lost
to what transcendent frightening inner pleasure
I can only imagine must have justified

those much-reported recent executions on the grounds.
But the thing about out-of-it and getting-off
was ever interruption. Take Kublai Khan.

Take this strip mounded hard above the wetland
and follow it to the island of gas pumps
one local dreamer established in real-life concrete and neon:

the video arcade, the auto wash, the colossal
flag he'd raised as monument
to his desperate meditation on Vietnam

only to have it ordered down, so many cars
full of midnight's stoned astonished pilots
had been distracted and diverted into the pole.

Piece of the Way

Too much to ask for the whole journey.
It was just that starting out together
I had badgered from my mother,
a quarter mile of whooping bugaloo to the bridge,
after which my pal went on, and I turned
from the sun and came back booting a clod
until, as he always did,
Miles Winton's incorrigible mongrel
spurted up from the ditchbank
like a flame turned inside out,
sleek black to the bone with rage
he'd always hold audibly at shoulder height
until, measuring my steps, I had tiptoed
past, and him behind me, still growling
as he leaked back into the shadows,
and turned into a stone or reaping machine,
but now the house before me was dark.
That was where my father would go
some nights, when a woman would arrive,
saying one or another of the grown boys
had gotten drunk and had the old man
down on the floor, and was about to beat
him to death with the broken leg of a chair
if my father would not come, and quick.
I passed, watchful, but not afraid,
for I knew that soon the dozen children,
cotton-headed, with twin jade sprigs
yo-yoing from the nostrils, would rush

out to hold up the youngest of the brood,
a tot they'd taught to say one word, *goddam.*
This was ordinary stuff, going home.
Farther down the road, I'd turn,
hearing a skillet or something bang against a wall,
and then the wailing and screech
that opened like a stone. No such thing
that I had ever heard made that noise.

Devil's Cellar

The inside *out-there* of the autumn woods,
unmarked bluffs in the gathering habits
of squirrels, stoppered rustlings, silences
where the human cologne buds
predation in the nostril of a doe,

sanctum sanctorum of mossy ledges,
and deep in the water under the water,
the farther opening into the cavern
that once passed for the subconscious,
for as I passed above, I thought I heard,

far below the boulders of the dry
creekbed, the voices of lost tribes
hearkening to the abiding troll
to turn the omphalos inside out
and unseal the ledger of arrearages

inked everywhere underground
since the settlers' hogsheads dragged
through the Cumberland Gap.
Also, down there beneath me,
old Bascomb Wilcutt had said there was

a bark canoe, stone weapons and tools,
a skin suit stretched out on a rock,
if only one could find the entrance.

But, as I said, the tribe was lost,
and obviously as always of such

a sudden, catastrophic, mysterious
agent of change as compels
the teenage skeptic to the immediate
apprehension of the works
of gods underestimated or no longer revered.

The Masters

When I began someone had already described
all the thoughts that might be suggested
by roots, what it is to go alone cold in twilight
down a country road past a cemetery,
all the ideas that were like leaves and boles,
all the dreams men had in factories,
and all the metaphors of mirrors and shadows.

Someone had used up all the women
with one arm and all the men with one eye,
and everything in the dump had been put
on paper and thrown into the dump
under other papers covered with the same words:
all the ways of smiling and drying one's hair;
all the unconscious, subliminal gestures

of pawnbrokers, short-order cooks, and stutterers
had been registered in the hallmark of sighs
and the museum of frowns; all the public
victories in private ruins had been ordained
in the scholarly journals and little magazines.
Both the plowed field and the barn
bursting with alfalfa had been set against

the works of Duke Ellington and Guglielmo
Marconi. No pixel of the ideal page
was not black with the traffic
of iambs, spondees, and double dactyls.

All the ways a tree might be said to speak
to a woman grieving the death of a child
had been claimed, purloined, reclaimed,

and readapted for pianos and violins.
All the words that had come into the language
in the last five years and all the styles
of exploiting one's knowledge of Latin.
Brake fluid, I thought, perhaps brake fluid,
but it was the age of tack and guy wires.

I would have to write a good pine tree
before I could walk the page recklessly,
missing the masters, but bolstered
by their absence, in it for the long haul
as if no poem had been made yet,
as if the poetry did not matter at all.

It Must Be Abstract

I think the here-and-there-heel-to-toe-right-
and-left-foot mobile geometry
of any walk contains all walks,

from Master Lonely's prodding forward
the aboriginal vacuums of his shadow
to old Waffle Thighs' meditative wobbling

to the teeter-totter brink of the bus stop;
all there, different mindsets and weathers,
the march seeded in the toddling to the pot;

and every walk in the progression
of years is less here and more there
where one has been or is going,

past the sensational temptations of stalls
where polished apples have been laid out on a table;
and all of it a piece of the way:

the long moment of a face looked into
and back there already, pierced
by the sounds of horns and the diesel

attar of buses; and the shorter moment
cuffed in the blurting of peripheries:
appearances of birds, or a fight

flickering out of the shadow of an alley,
to be cited later and drawn out,
so eventually every place resolves

in gaze, hum, and life-speed of walking.
And the great movement called Romance
continues as a vision that will survive us,

as a verb survives its nouns, as new
lovers come with picnics to an old cemetery.
It is all there, unfinished and complete.

The Music of Repose

A cat whines in the night, scat and vaudeville,
and the larger music,
which contains all sounds and silences,
and which one rarely notices,
either because its rhythms occur too quickly
or it takes centuries for the harmonies to resolve,
emerges from the cry.

The woven rope of many songs
that marks a single life
hangs there, knotted by interruptions.
The Hardy Boys had hardly entered
the secret passageway
when my mother's voice called me
to the unhoed garden, the unmown lawn.
The old woman, my great-aunt Cordelia—
who in September had let me read
the ancient love letters boxed in her attic
and promised to show me a gold coin
dug up in her garden—
caught pneumonia in October and died.

Cat-whine, love cry, the bird
that makes the noise *rio rio rio*
again and again. The saddest song I know
is "Just a Closer Walk with Thee."
A band played it as we linked arms at the Maple Leaf Bar
and marched, four hundred souls,
swaying down Oak Street in consecutive columns.

And the one in front of us all,
the little brilliant alcoholic,
our teacher, who had lived
so bravely and unwisely,
who had quoted Keats and stood on tables
to play on a tiny bamboo flute
"Raindrops Keep Falling on My Head,"
sent out a wire of delicate spiritual
lightning from his Tupperware urn.

My grandmother, by playing softly
on her piano "Just As I Am,"
intended to break down our flintiness
and self-absorption and dissolve
the moral calcium
that had hardened our hearts.
So the fingers on the horns
seemed to be pushing us.

Then the music stopped. Some
ordered Tom Collins on the rocks.
Some flirted as they wiped their eyes.
Then we went on, buoyant,
in keeping with tradition,
the band jigging and highstepping
to an up-tempo rendition
of "When the Saints Go Marching In."
Back at the Maple Leaf, many
gave eulogies or read poems.

My friend found the happiness
of friends unbearable. "This
fucking asshole world," he liked to say
when he was not praising sloth,
lechery, degradation, nympholepsy,
and dipsomania, or poking
his pointing finger through his fly
to terrify the ones who pretended
to be something they weren't.

Consciousness and mortality:
it got to be a competition between us
two great stooges of music
to hear more in less. By the end,
he'd won, hands down. Voltage
hummed his favorite tune.
He was so busy dying
he couldn't cry for dancing.

Brains

When I moved in with her I thought, Now
I won't have to look it up:
rubidium, Lionel Trilling, the fourth-
longest river in Brazil.
The lunar mountain ranges
zoomed in. Zygotes and paramecia
made themselves known. She
could cook a mean boeuf bourguignon,
then rank the leading authorities
on the aspiration of the *h*
or mystical tenses of Latin verbs.
But you are so creative, there's
not a creative bone in my body,
she would say, when I insisted
before friends we had recently met
that not I but she was the brain.
Now that she is gone,
now I can feel secure, one
thought sending another
down through the foggy
databases, the fractures,
and the unions. Here boy,
I whistle to the dog of my thoughts.
I am thinking how,
before I lived with her,
I was known as the brain,
but I valued the heart more than the brain,
and more than the heart,
the flag of the erogenous zones.
Loving me was like patriotism,

but I was not fit to live with her.
I knew, when she began to chant
and burn incense to the Asian saints,
I did not know her secret anything.
Still, I had ideas, insights,
a brain like the world's mute,
lightning-soldered, accidental
intelligence. With that same
brain now I hold our ill-starred,
incompatible visions
of happiness and tragedy.
Yet when I need to know
how spinnerets work
or the distance to Alpha Centauri,
I think of her, not for long
or at any depth, or what
she was, but the last
compliment that means anything
is the compliment to memory.

Nudes

1

I was not more than five. A girl in the fields
had shown me what girls have down there,
but only a glimpse before our parents were
around us with their hoes, so for all the years
of childhood and on into adolescence, I had
only that one clue, and nothing to do with it
but read, pouring myself into the classics,
prying at the boulders of titles that seemed apt.
The Secret Garden? The Anatomy of Melancholy?
In the glass office at the back of the stacks,
Mrs. Floyd Baumgardner, our skunk-haired
Daughters of the Confederacy bibliophile,
clipped genitalia throughout the Renaissance
while I glossed our badly printed local daily.
The buxom starlets in the drive-in ads,
when I looked closely, would turn to dots.

2

The power to shock is a quality of modesty.
An ex-Jesuit took me to my first titty bar.
I wanted vision. Also, I wanted to chat.
"My name is Fancy," she said, "and I am going
to dance for you." Well, that is what they do
down here, coming to the pink verge without
ever shedding that last ribbon of flimsy silk,
that sequined picket line of smiling evangelists,

which is their only raiment and fashion.
But where did she come from, and how to
this end, a grown woman in a black string,
not bad looking, from what I could see,
with good bones, and the actual breasts.
When I asked her last name, she said, "Strawberries."

3

Eve, Helen of Troy, Mary, then Fatima:
the oldest man at the bachelor party, I
am not so old that I do not remember.
When she pranced out in the letter sweater,
it was eighth grade again, the day
of the test on South America, the day
of the night of the county basketball finals
when Sally, the sprite a desk ahead of me,
would leap bountifully in her great cheer
and leap also in the fantasy life, making
the names of the rivers all run together.

4

The lap dancer's dress-up nudity is a doll.
Geisha. Self-artifice. Professional candor.
The way the stereotypical male poet's penis
is a feathered quill or mechanical pencil
and he's rewriting *Hansel and Gretel*.

Also, she's childhood's fate whispering,
"Rodney, don't you remember me?
Michelle. We met at Ron's." I don't.
But blush a blush that evolves from
John Calvin, and watch her squirm.
Part Mata Hari, part alma mater,
her straddling act camouflages
some chatter about her newest daughter.
Her privates against mine like that,
young men watching. Such is fame.

Bufus

We have founded a new kind of frog:
three-legged, one-eyed; or one-legged with three
eyes. Hops backward. Spongiform
tentacles creep its spine. Odd
to describe, like tubing around the heart,
an off *la* in the elemental rag.

Is Earth already whacked? How
address a prayer: "God, Jr."? "Ms. God"?
The iron heats, the waffles pop.
But grace stings the meat. What a strange
duffel brother esophagus unpacks.
Taste quick. It's sewage down a pipe.

Void once meant filth. Frogs hopped
what grew from it. Now the jig's up.
Elimination spawns a myth.
Frogs lollygag under a rainbow
scrim of antifreeze and PCPs
or leap to prophets in songs.

Cinema sci-fi loves anthro-frogs,
orange planets of tight clothing
where cyber-sleuths glibly concoct
the quantum physics of a hop.
Ideal frogs are rainforest cancer cures.
The default frog's a caricature.

The default human's real. But how
weird to live in a body: looking out

but always staying in, not
knowing what's there and not,
and all the while beating against
the limits of perception like a moth.

I'm happiest, froglike, in a tub,
ballooning a wash of ticklish bubbles.
Money swallows men and excretes cartoons.
Make everything simple. Water's
the central dodge. Everything
shed comes back as drinking water.

Fidelity

Two walks running, the big hill stopping him,
        we portaged him home in the truck.
Dr. K's prognosis, inoperable tumor, started the drip.
        Dog mourning was a form of guilt:

For each morning he had carried the news in his mouth,
        for he sat beside me as I composed drafts
        of poems that blundered unerringly
until he corrected them with a remonstrative wag;

        For he had led me through briars
for all the grand criminal lark of his puppyhood,
        whirling to taunt, barking and bolting
                each time I came near

until, at last, I seized him by the collar and whipped him
                with a stick, for he might have died
                on the bumper of a passing Volvo
                or been dognapped by the laboratories

        had I not stepped forth with such mastery
that never in all his life would he come to me outside
                even when I held out the salt
                cordial of liver chips. So he was mine.

        But the man or woman who dies far off,
        and the boy murdered by his stepfather:
                why should these yip or bark
                while a dog speaks in a human voice?

To be ruled by proximity was fine in the dark.
It shrank brute race to friendlier tribe.
Now shortsightedness is the crime.
We have faced ourselves. And are the other side.

Doggy guilt refines this bafflement:
an awareness of an awareness of an awareness,
vaguely treasured, obliquely felt
in the almost Pidgin American of a bark.

"Bad dog," I'd say when he'd run off.
It had about as much effect as prayer.
The individual in our pack, he taught us whim.
He dogs us now who humaned him.

Bones with No Meat on Them

Dark, not glum, it's like that here. Last night
I heard two animals struggling in the bush
and feared the stars. Then silence prophesied.
This morning was a take. Pancakes, blueberries.
I sunned on the deck, practicing Nirvana,
conjuring texts like *The Postmodernist Outdoorsman,*
or rehashing scenes from life, bit parts
played by accidents and passing obsessions.
It had been a good life, if that was mine.
It didn't take its cues from death. It thrived.
Meanwhile, the general static of animal
well-being kept this ineluctable Morse leaping
down the spine, *to eat, to fuck, to sleep,*
like an architect's illustration of a discotheque
where the Puritan-packed insulation
had frayed a little from the sublime.
Oh I thought of big things, too: the big
bang, black holes, and global warming,
but, given recent misthrusts, impertinence
might turn out to be a plus, like jettisoning
less, deciding not to work, or declining
to reproduce. I mean, large questions lurk,
but little ones make friends. At any rate,
clarity and articulation hold. If a man
sets out to be a visionary, he has to get
what he sees before the worms bind it
back to the invisible source. For the lucky
there's no choice, only a besieged
gaze through the polyhedral eye
of what happy staff of the self happen

to be around that day. It's a rat.
Then it's a principle. You show it
to your children if you love them.
What happened is not a thing you hide.

Four

A Photograph in an Old Anthology

At Pier 1 you can still see
the very wicker chair
in which Pound was photographed,
with a white flame for hair
and Ezekiel eyes: an image
that goes with tea and empire
and suggests a quiet dignity,
a Confucian repose;
though he also might
have been shown monocled,
in the khakis that Banana Republic sells now,
to signify the fascist and the crank.

I saw it when I was nineteen,
when many poets posed
with berets askance
or pipes wafting to the heavens:
abominable pretensions
I thought at the time;
though I had been myself
for the better part of a year
growing my hair long
and tilting a gold pair
of granny glasses halfway
down my nose to affect
the intense nonchalance
of John Lennon or Roger McGuinn.

What's vaster than nostalgia?
Hypocrisy. The age launched

from a headshop — pea coats
molting into Nehru jackets, Republicans
combing their hair straight back,
Democrats sweeping it
forward and to the side —
everyone trying to become
someone else, unsuccessfully,
and the failure a part
of the success: Kafka
wanting to sound like Dickens.

What decorates a man? The old
ape-secret mystique — reared
on pride, foundering on hubris —
works its mojo on the lam.
Pound's crazy, brilliant bible
still lights a seminar. Rapture
and humiliation: one cock
is skewered on another's talons.
Every man's an invisible public.
Narcissus always sees another.
As others saw me, let me see myself:
posturing on the quad with some
Emma Goldman Alabama belle
and suffering to hear myself
compared to Teddy Roosevelt.

Ten Sighs from a Sabbatical

1

Let loose. Lists into ashes. Tasks into stones.
In lethargy I revise myself. I loiter in the lily's canal.
Time to mood-walk among obsolete resolutions.
To drain rhetoric to all that does not speak and cannot listen.
Hello, thistle. What do horses hear?
A nap cleans me like a tooth. Mere duty rocks the hours.
The brain's self-whispering brushes the conscious event.
The face of a good friend is a breast.
A call comes in on the switchboard of the birds.
I swivel and skitter, a potato thrown through a warehouse.
I am injected with dream questions.
Instruct me, heavenly recipe for the worms.
How long must I be buried before I am done?
Rub me right, rule me, sweet other.
I'm old wood and new string.
I can only be an animal through this violin.

2

Who speaks now as if subject and predicate decree the world?
The trees were locked up, but have broken out.
I trail off down the sidewalk of an afterthought.
Only a busted cycle, Lord, a gleam spirited to rust.
What litters of darkness televisions own.
I'm a punched ticket swaddled by lint.
Come, eavesdroppers, hear the foreplay of obsessions.
A tsk-tsking, with a dumpty-do for variation.
Who else sits here, blues-measled, lonesome afternoons,
looking up follicle and Warren G. Harding
in *Compton's Illustrated Encyclopedia*?
Are you better than once, lightest foreshadowing?
Are you the largest amygdala in homeroom?

3

Pilgrim, what good there is for you to see
finds you. You don't have to look for it.
A lily trembles by a spring-fed brook.
Live children dream. A tax accountant
does a glum impression of Charlie Chan.
I'm off this year, dally to your dilly, yang
to your yin, but let me visit the office
once, friends open their mouths
to show the scars of humorectomies.
Why? Who's not wronged? Go cut a switch,
my own sweet mama used to say, and me,
I'd bring back a reed while my smarter
sister would present a gnarl of thorns.
But there's a glitch in utter victimhood.
The wronged-by-men-and-women face down
the wronged-by-God. Walk fast or run.
All verse writers moan, Too late, and zoom!
We're poster children for the irony telethon.

4

But oh to have come up with something new:
a minor amendment to a hairdo,
a twitch in a phrase, or chevron on shirt.
The will of others must be sidestepped after all.
If one is to reach into the pocket and bring up
like a magician's rabbit the gold eggs of the future,
one needs a tongue ring, earring, or mustache,
though in the case of bards, what dumb malaise
and spiritual laryngitis leave may be only
the aboard-saying panic and subliminal love sigh
of the greased consonants turning among vowels.
"Stretch out," they seem to say, "lay it all down
here in the seeds of the twenty-first century,
in the United States of America," and, "Baby, baby."

5

The great man, head like a cauliflower, addressed our poems
Thursday mornings, pontificating between coughing jags.
And what he said: "History includes you in this small way."
And what he meant: "Don't wake me up."
He who had sat with Cummings, Hart Crane, and Pound.

And what he remembered of all his time with Eliot:
"He never said anything stupid. He never made a mistake."

 "Why are you doing this?" I asked, the one time we were alone.
"I'm giving my wife a horse or a swimming pool."

Cummings was a gentleman. Pound was genuinely batty
and believed himself Christ. Randall was jealous of Cal.
"Cal should be exonerated for what he's writing now."

He skewered Mallarmé: "A short poet with a long tail."
Then hacked at himself: "A quarrel with imitations."

He liked my poems best. Not much. I asked one other thing:

"After all these years, and books, what do you think of poetry?"

"I loathe and detest it."

6

The dead, when they are recent, are as good
as they will ever be. They do not bicker
or take the biggest share. They lie in state,
as well groomed and polite as ambassadors.
Done with the future, they hold to the past.
Soon enough it will be different, heavenly host,
God's moles, God's worms, God's nematodes,
Gabriels and Saint Peters of putrefaction: hello.
Blooms praise meat. But now an interlude. Now,
as never in elegies, the living prefer the living.

7

My father, for all my childhood, would oppose
my sighs as others might object to profanity.
If I had finished splitting a pile of logs
or loading a truck of hay into the barn,
I had only to lean back, inhale a great gulp
of air and expel it with an undiminished *whew,*
and there he was like Marcus Aurelius.
Long I held tight, but now I give out
and go down the cleansing breath
dead-legged and bath-headed with joy.

8

Let loose. Lists into ashes. Tasks into stones.
Do the dead still dispatch scouts? Only
lunatics see angels. Surrealism's old-timey.
After fifty, the men in my family doze off,
even passionately making a point, intensity
of eyes coming down on you like a wake—
you start to answer, and we're off
in the slack-jawed, log-sawing sublime.
This clear gift descends on us like water.
Thunder brings out our highest power.

9

Release is better than ecstasy, downglide
peeled from the resistance of the living,
sockfoot in the meridian of twilight.
What picked the brain like a morel?
The honesty of things calls silently. Minutes
of committee meetings, doodlings
and scribblings make the soul's holy writ.
The rain says, Go and study with the birds.

10

It doesn't take much. Beautiful platitude:
All is delusion. In the right dark,
and if you are ignorant, brother,
a goose sounds like a coyote.
I'm looking for something a wren will approve.
One leak from the unlockable sea.
What's truer than fiction when it moves?
The peach in my own armflesh
makes me an agent of the sublime.

Wood

Having denied the obsolescence of the Holy Trinity and the disappear-
ance of the soul, he prayed early and went out in short sleeves to split the
green hickory logs. His steady popping and muscular pleasure with the
ax seemed kin to pulling taffy or polishing brass, and his rhythm did not
gather or squinch, even when the blade glanced or stuck in a dark knot
at the heart. Flowing and flying chips and sparks. The soul and the log,
he'd balance these the way come summer he'd hold himself aloft on the
central beam where the rafters meet and figure lengths, or after dinner,
solve with his left hand some easy mystery of the piano. The kind of
musician who served as entertainment before radio, a great admirer of
Fanny J. Crosby, blind composer of minor hymns, a composer himself,
a singer, not especially talented, but happy with his talent.

The Harvest King

That he had read and traveled much gave credence
to what he said, riding in the wagon beside us
while we pulled corn or bucked hay. Though
his blow-by-blow analysis of the effects
of tribal jostlings in the Middle East
on the price of oil helped little in the crib,
still he arrived each year at harvest,
not settled in yet when he began digging
at the communal feed, benign parasite
remarked on and tolerated for his conversation.

Professor of fields, sweat lectured with him.
Entomology subsumed ideology. He redacted
our mountains to foothills, but added
caves, the dream of limestone that primed
our spelunking in the depths. His own life
he spoke of rarely, walking the voluble
pleasure of his post-meal cigarette:
a reluctant fiancée, a weak and sickly child
bullied by classmates long dead, himself
surviving by moderation, victorious in longevity.

Going

From the bootlegger's shanty at Five Points
to the swing sets in the Falkville schoolyard,
the road went underwater, which made
our twice-a-day bus rides through the bottoms

dead ringers for those geography tests
when I'd wonder if I'd studied enough,
guessing the brain's good dog might send up
Utah when I'd sent down for Nevada.

This was also the biblical road,
flood-fleshed with bedwettings and cold sweat.
It clarified distinctions between tests:
fake true-or-false was wilting mimeograph;

real true-or-false was marked on the rail
where a neighbor girl, returning from a dance,
had flunked the bridge and fueled a sermon.
Geography turned to philosophy if we stalled,

and while the engine turned, some prayed,
some leapt up jeering, and would be chastised
mildly and then forgiven. Most tolerant of men,
Fred Jenkins, the shell-shocked veteran, drove.

Pompadour

It was timely like a scab. It went out-of-date.
But what will endure is not a question
that burns with the same pizzazz
as when cowlicks crested in the barber's chair.

My eyes sank to Granville Wallace
shining a boot or climbed spruce
paneling to a poster of classic haircuts
that had stuck since the Great Depression.

Studying it, I thought the bald would die.
And they did. Plywood bandaged the stores.
Our final surgeon-barber was the bank.
Some principle of timeliness remains

after wars and words of great speeches.
My first thought of history was the
history of haircuts. Haircuts toeing
the line between the living and the dead.

The one with the part in the middle
was already the exclusive purview of urban pets
and would have had the look
of Valentino if I had seen him yet.

The Roommate, 1969

What I thought is not important.
There was a gun in his hand.
He was angry, that much was clear.
And drunk. I had hurt him,

without meaning to, and now,
once more, he meant to tell me
what he'd done in the war, and to ask
how I'd survived the summer of love.

I had just turned twenty years old.
I did not know much of anything
about what a boy might have to say
in order to live into manhood.

Please? Listen? I had written
a few essays, a couple of stories.
I had never prayed to a man,
and then he held it up to me:

a little .22 revolver. Not that he
would have used it. He was already
a Buddhist then. He didn't
point it at me. He showed it to me.

Paradise

Paradise was a vision after a pill,
so I walked, dream-letting
among condemned houses, eyeing
with light-giving gold
each cornice and column, each cantilever
of intelligent labor shining
with cathedral and castle fire.

And entered history, came what
seemed two thousand years
down corridors of long-haired
Old Testament prophets.
Though, of course, it was just
the usual hippies, the usual
Tuscaloosa sidewalk, a step
and step, and in her yard,
my landlady waving her hands.

Whining, whining, always whining,
but this time like a wall —
"My furniture," she cried.
"The crane dropped it
as they were unloading the train."
Then I saw it, boxed
and scattered on the porch:
dressers and chairs in smithereens,
a smashed highboy, a lamp —

Why think of it now? In June
I moved, and never visited,

never returned. Spells die
like things: *all of a sudden,*
as children like to jump-
start the ends of tales: lights
off in fairyland, the trance
gone, the moment stubbed—

And is nothing, a slub or rip
in the fabric of one year.
The same year a man leapt
through the window of a cafeteria
and, bleeding, cried, "I'm Jesus Christ.
I forgive you." Nothing,
only what it was, but her voice
like a hook grappling
for a drowned boy, and the net
through her hair like veins,
and under those veins the skull.

Into which I thought I saw—what?
That she was there, an other,
not myself, not this remnant
that I carry now, this strand
of dangling charms,
each the death's head
of another time, shrink-wrapped
on the point of vanishing.

Well. I am slow. It has taken me
nearly fifty years to believe

that the world is real.
But what lasts in the brain
must mean something simple,
drawn like the soil in an oak,
known because lived through.
Knowledge comes with absence.
Paradise is the story of a ruin.

Five

Divine Love

for Reverend Louie Skipper

1

What they called the temple was a dingy bungalow
where a few were always gathered, never far above

the tenuous grip of levitation, but randy for the depths
innumerable of the *Bhagavad Gita* and *I Ching,*

wisdom being a mystique all its own, with the same
obsessive-compulsive trigger as photography or chess,

though the meat inside the mystery puff is nearly
always sex. I used to hang there, catch-as-catch-can,

a stone agnostic among Sufis and Sufi poseurs,
and the sheikh — Ricky was his name — would sneak

over the fence when there were parties
and quaff a manhattan. Purity on furlough.

Chuckling at jokes. One spirit trumping another.
While his flock envisioned silence and auditioned dark.

But give them this: abundant friendliness, tolerance.
The group was into fingerpicking and had good pot.

2

Bless duplicity in all things: reverence of the individual
followed by disdain; the outcast, followed by his tribe.

Bless public tolerance. And living masks. The truth
will come out of a man, but not through the mouth.

The hawk, with its lucid speculation, has flown.
The interior auctioneer has lost his voice.

And now that everything has been sold,
the girl who starved herself down to the bone

and the man who gave himself repeated enemas
in the sealed ward above the x-ray machines

aren't such mysteries after all. I am tired
of the same sheep and the same farm. Infinite

accident rules science; theorem and egos pop!
Now the long face of my thought stares back at me,

with little wads clumped on the shaving cuts.
So I was blessed. Lacking anger, I was given vanity.

3

There is a great light in self-knowledge,
but the real joy for any honest kid
comes from pretending to be
someone with a foreign accent
whose life doesn't matter in the least.
Then it will be over by supper, will it?
The amalgamated self will divest
one by one its incorporeal holdings.
Banjo man will molt his twang.
Faulty nuclear reactor man will zap
back into a natural American English,
and our little kipper can gargle,
spit, slip on those bunny slippers,
and command Mum to uneasily read
of Einstein, ebola, typhus, and anthrax.

4

For God so loved the world, but what about his son?
was a question I asked myself repeatedly growing up
in north Alabama, for Jesus was never far from us,

a good person, always sticking up for the downtrodden,
healing the lame, or nailing a slam-dunk proverb.
He was that kind of guy. Compassionate. Crafty.

He could walk on water and turn water to wine.
Even stretched on the cross, spears in his side,
you could see he would rise, but what kind of father

would wait three days to bring a son back to life?
I would ask my seventh-grade teacher, Mr. Prater.
And even when I had grown and created my own life,

I would ask, as a chicken leg was being raised
to a mouth or a watermelon circled by a gnat,
Didn't he make those days and have foreknowledge?

Such was my block, my fog in the air around heaven.
Oh a few of the distant cousins would argue:
it must have been, long ago, a different thing,

with some occasional alterations in the natural order.
The dead came back to life, wings emerged from fire.
Select individuals might suddenly drift skyward.

Gravity didn't work all the time. Sometimes
diseases that had been perfectly lethal failed.
Persons got transformed into other substances.

Other species were fertilized by divine sperm.
This went on and on. And gradually passed.
The age of miracles, and the belief in miracles.

Not at once, but over years, as leaves dry to grist,
as a pump rusts and the fans of a windmill rot.
Faith goes on silently like questions in the dark.

The hospital is Mercy. The cemetery is Pleasant.
The good shepherd moves calmly among his flock.
For a child who whispers, *forever and ever and ever,*

belief shines briefly, from the other side of the river.
Hard not to see how worship leads to the cross.
Hard not to have unrealistic expectations of a god.

5

But life's no icon. Childhood's no scar. Boy-world's
an evolving call to arms. Beneath the clangor
of imaginary swords, my sister sautéed bugs.
Me, I did silent impressions of Jehovah.
Dreams shed natural wonders, and the truth got lied
while the weather chorused low in soprano.
Did I have a heart? Did I pace soulfully in the clouds?
Sometimes I wanted to speak like a real guy,
so an Elvis or a Muddy Waters might suit up in an embryo.

But let me as much as blink, wheelchairs rolled off porches
all over Alabama, fires furled, sexes got mixed up.
Now I hold my voice. The angels are on strike.
As it was in the beginning, so it will be
amalgamated and recycled in *The Star*.
Small world, there is more time than the world's time
when you are a god. Oh it gets to be too much
to love, but the good part is, presto, a proton
here, a muon there, history's revised: fate's my alibi.

6

Wondrous and antique to craft from pluck
and perseverence sixty years of married love,

but to smith a really mean dalliance takes guts,
a wild loiter outside the quotidian waste of time.

The thingness falls from things. There's tonic
in sunsets for the bewildering human palate:

but wander the double lie and exponential
pain of lovers, you come to passion,

ground zero of religion and art. Meanwhile,
the soul's like helium. It requires a mask.

Expressionism's already ancient now:
Shiva up to her arms in blood. The barely

living gods, Zeus and Leda in ecstasy,
masquerading as the midtown bus.

7

In my fiftieth year, I narrowed to a deep funk:
the self infected with rage, the self in self-lust.
Self-census requires the study of a lot:

e.g., was you thinking, or was you thought?
To improve decisions, internalize the people you imagine
you admire and have them vote. As for values,

beauty's tops. Self-denial gets you brownie points.
The secondary depths of Christianity strike
one last: forbear, suffer; and when you fall in love,

each potential beloved's like a hostel, occupied.
But all divinity bores God, especially her own.
I like comedy more than tragedy, light more than dark,

and prefer music to the tedious arts.
If my Jesus were personal, he'd be Harpo Marx.
Holy days are days off. Shake, then. Try

not to get stirred up. Fiction's inside like faith.
It doesn't count unless you believe it, and
you don't have to know it for it to be the truth.

8

Even if I was sick, my covenant was with the flesh:
a fruit lover, a shaker-down of apples and mangoes,
an avid remembrancer of breast and inner thigh,
in flavors and favors blessed, appreciating trees,
in all pleasures slightly sophisticated, ready,
expecting the letdown and relishing the peaks.
Strawberry and rhubarb, lamb and cucumber.
All my better nature was nerved like a tongue.

Lover of people (some), I did not want my children in a church,
at one, in lovely song, with wisdoms ready-made.
Let them rinse and perm their own halos.
Of my own church rearing, I remember the dark
after long services, racing between cars,
the sanctuary quiet that had been so recently thralled
to joyful tears. Good people, my family loved the Lord.
I praise their church, apse and steeple of the word.

9

What does a man love that he should not perish?
A myth, a thing that does not exist.
A compass between fear and wish.
Omnium-gatherum, theological jellyfish
propelling itself by heavenly quotes
through the murky latter-day summary
of *Science of Eternity for Dummies*.

Why do stars shrink from the eyes at twilight?
I, too, searched for something in a book.
As if infinity were not enough
and particle-splitters groping for some void-
proof nano-being evanescent as the soul
might pack all that we need to know
in the sham and shore noise of a word.

Music says more. Logic's gospel. Time
to recast the stories that didn't work.
The living pray for the living to live.
Not for heaven's citherns and palms.
But from the central hub, the crucial lust,
you may go easily, to darkness given,
and you do not have to earn your oblivion.

Moses

Moses is massive, as Michelangelo sculpted him for the tomb
     of Pope Julius II,
looking off to the side in outward vigilance while inwardly
     descending:
the face of a judge with the body of a mechanic or teamster;
     a fine delicacy of veins,
a muscular trauma in the stone, he seems to hide in revelation
     and exalt while suffering.

Clinton is six-three; Bush Senior was a little shorter, unless
     Clinton stood in platform shoes
while they debated. Dukakis lost to Senior, not because of
     Willie Horton but because
he was five-eight and, in the lethal advertisement, helmeted,
     waving giddily from the tank,
he resembles a peripatetic spud, as though the divine seamstress
     had run out of material
and attached the body of a presumptuous child to the brain
     of a grown man. A mistake. Though

only blemish suggests God to the cynic — a botch, a humanizing
     crack in the stone.
There must be terror. And Moses was tongue-tied. His brother
     spoke for him. So the law
opened, veiled in mystique, graven of a grave height and distance,
     and in this,
I am convinced, there is a secret wisdom, a fiction they must
     never know is fiction.
That Moses was himself Sinai: that is Michelangelo's secret.

The image accomplishes
more. It bares the loneliness of a man who has seen God.

Mastery speaks for the design of politics, but politics is not art.
        Not usually.
Politics is like justice: blind, but less helpful, more forgiving.
        Art is mercilessly simple:
implicit everywhere one thing looks something like another,
        but more explicitly,
the thing itself, relieved by knowledgeable infusion, crafted,
        and distressed to beauty.
In Rome, you can see it now, in the basilica of San Pietro
        in Vincoli,
one of the few stones touched and improved by the human hand.

Song of Affirmation

From all races and nations, may the future
find among the legacies and approved minorities
a place for the ugly, weak, stupid, and small.

The call of the left-out starts from rusted trailers
in leeched back hollers and rat-infested flats
behind the broken glass of closed factories.

To all the uncoordinated, out-of-key, and color-blind
may there be given that distinguished paramour
who is neither cousin, sibling, nor child.

For the duck-footed and pigeon-toed
may there be phone numbers to call.
For everyone cross-eyed, harelipped,

gap-toothed, and lurching along on braces,
may there arise a position and delectation.
May there always come shelter

for the water-retentive and the aboriginally shy,
for the cowlicked and the bald, for all
the redheaded speckled ones, for the

snub-nosed and chinless. For those
covered with moles and coarse dark hairs,
for the pony boy and tiger woman,

may there be no recrimination or hatred.
May the afflicted, rejected, cheated,
and shorted regard without envy

the hale champion and queen of beauty.
The margin bequeaths hallelujah and song.
Gunfire and poison make the victim dance.

To live in a remission of enlightenment
is to be given a faith and an irony
whose end is praise: almighty is the God.